Rubber duckies, aren't they fine?
Which line shows us the answer, 9?

= 10

= 9

= 8

= 7

= 6

= 5

= 4

= 3

= 2

= 1

= 0

For Mim Galligan,
who is brave.
—J. M.

For my nephews, Hudson and Carter,
and their helping hands.
—C. P.

HOLIDAY HOUSE is registered in the U.S. Patent and Trademark Office.
Printed and Bound in March 2012 at Tien Wah Press, Johor Bahru, Johor, Malaysia.
www.holidayhouse.com
First Edition
1 3 5 7 9 10 8 6 4 2

Library of Congress Cataloging-in-Publication Data
Marzollo, Jean.
Help me learn subtraction / by Jean Marzollo ; photographs by Chad Phillips. — 1st American ed.
p. cm.
Audience: Ages 4-7.
ISBN 978-0-8234-2401-6 (hbk.)
1. Subtraction—Juvenile literature.
2. Counting-out rhymes—Juvenile literature.
I. Phillips, Chad, ill. II. Title.
QA115.M332 2012
513.2'12—dc23
2011046540

Help Me Learn Subtraction

by **Jean Marzollo**

photographs by

Chad Phillips

Holiday House / New York

3 birds look alive!

Add 2 more.
That makes _____ (5).

Three plus two is five.
$$3 + 2 = 5$$

That's not
subtraction.

That's
addition!

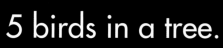

5 birds in a tree.

2 fly away.
That leaves _____ (3).

Five minus two
equals three.
5 − 2 = 3

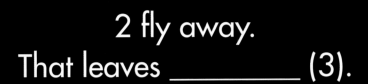

If 5 − 2 = 3,
does 3 + 2 = 5?

Yes! Subtraction
is the opposite
of addition.

6 shy dinosaurs don't know
what to do.

So 4 try to hide!
That leaves _____ (2).

$$\begin{array}{r} 6 \\ -\,4 \\ \hline 2 \end{array}$$

10 monsters looking fine!

1 folds down.
Still up? _____ (9)

$$10 - 1 = 9$$

Subtraction is a
takeaway action.

Correct!

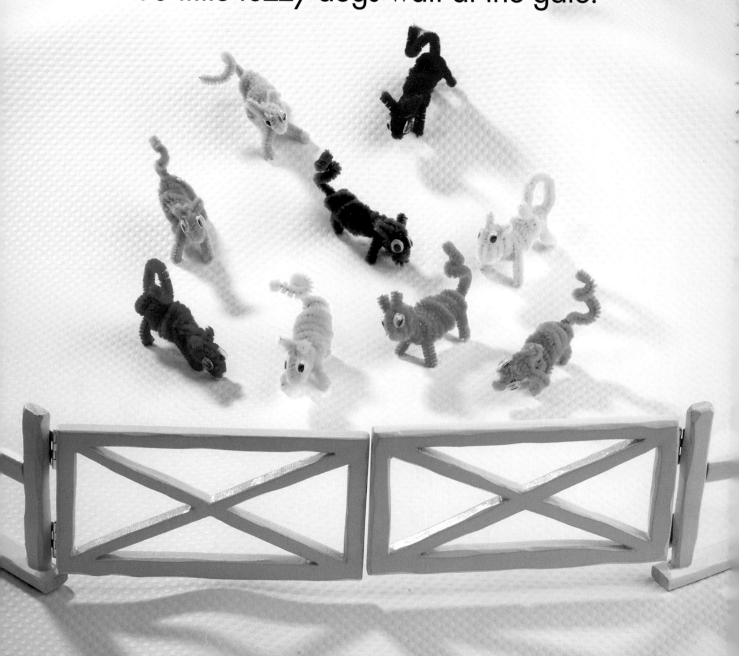

10 little fuzzy dogs wait at the gate.

If 2 go out,
how many still wait? _____ (8)

10 − 2 = 8

11 frogs race to the line!

How many hop over
to leave behind 9?

11 – ? = 9

13 pigs having fun.

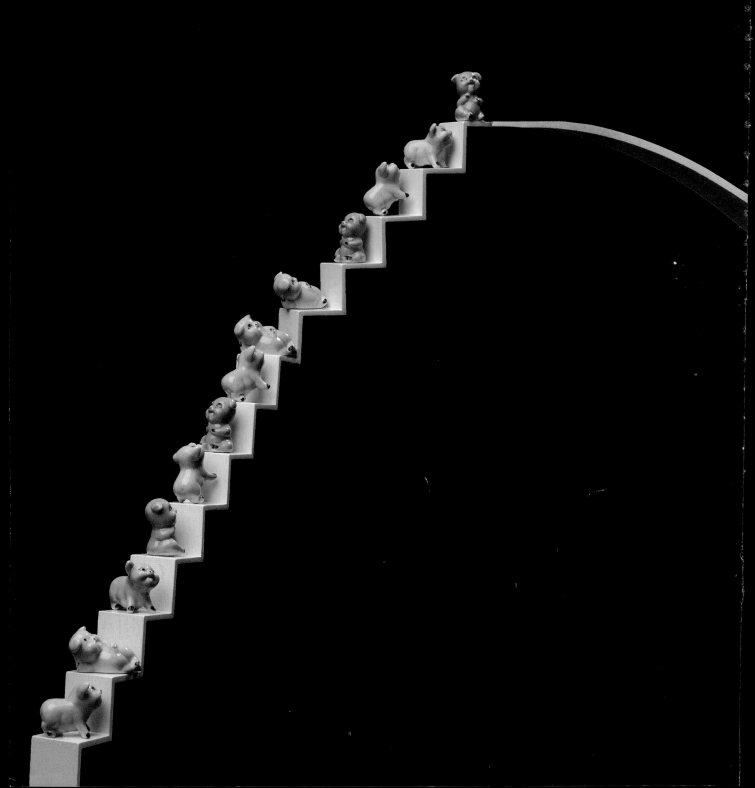

12 slide down.
On top?
Just _____ (1).

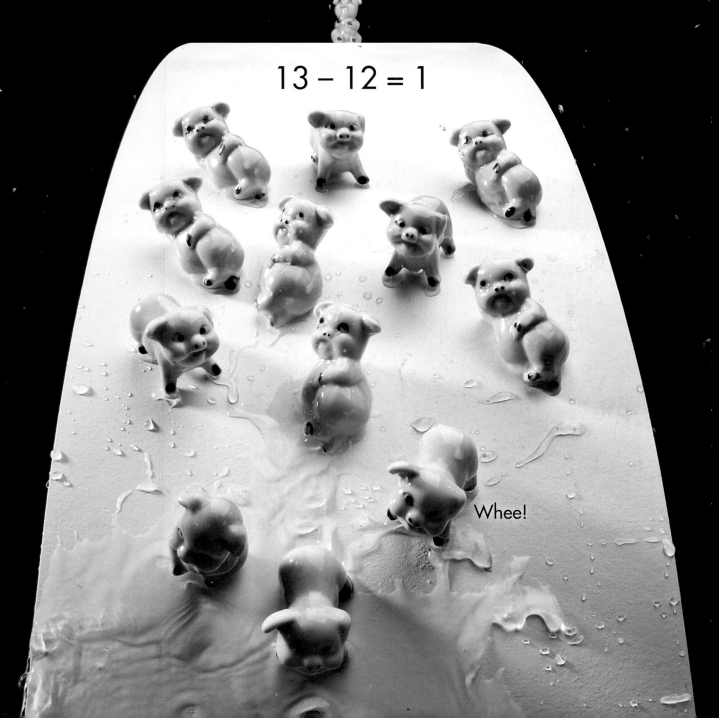

13 − 12 = 1

Whee!

Penguins play Subtraction Time!

Seven  minus two

7 − 2

Five  minus two

5 − 2

Three  minus one

3 − 1

Two  minus one

2 − 1

Here's their number sentence rhyme.

equals five
who like to dive.

= 5

equals three
for you and me.

= 3

equals two
who like the zoo.

= 2

equals one.
This is fun!

= 1

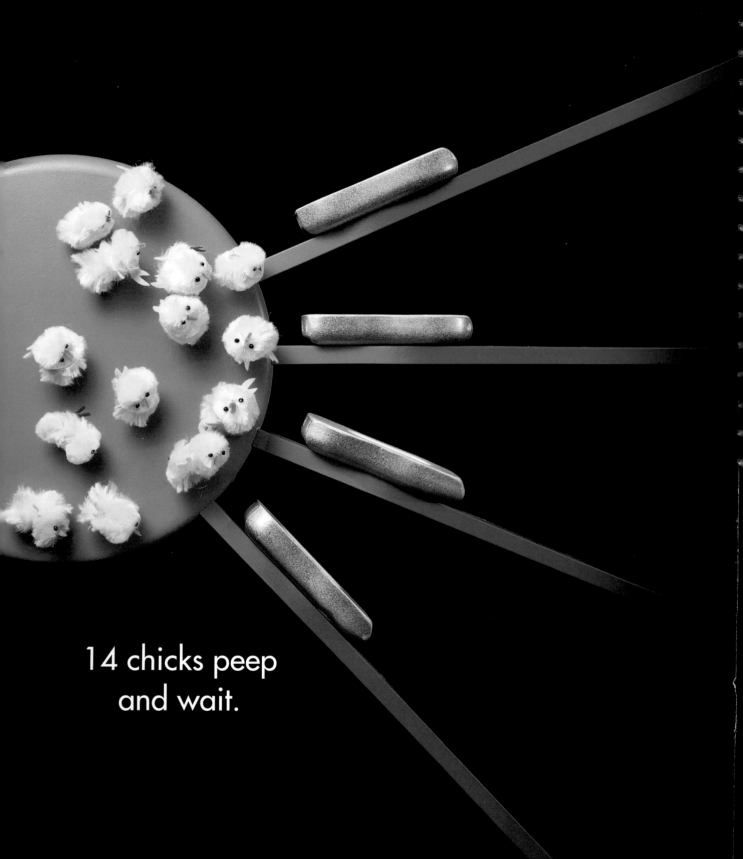

14 chicks peep
and wait.

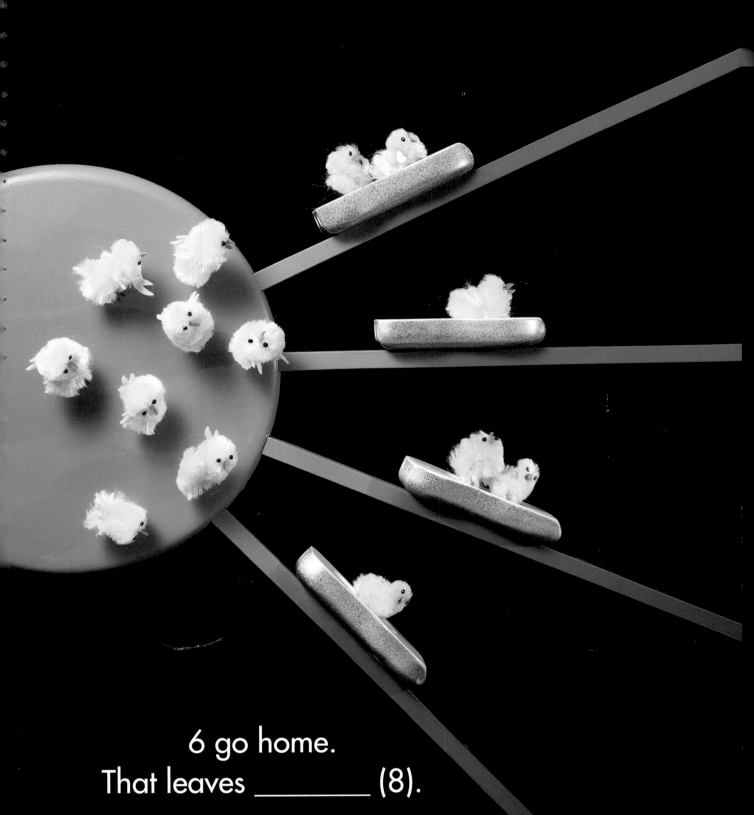

6 go home.
That leaves _____ (8).

14 − 6 = 8

8 chicks peep in the sun.

7 more go home.
That leaves _____ (1).

$$8 - 7 = 1$$

Now what? Turn the page!

The last one says,
"Peep! I'm a hero!
So I'll fly home."
That leaves _____ (0).

1
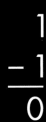
- 1
___
0

Where did
that plane
come from?

Maybe it
was a prize
for being so
patient.

Dear Parents and Teachers,

The purpose of this book is to help young children enjoy the experience of learning subtraction so that they will be ready to succeed in kindergarten and future grades.

Based on the Common Core State Standards, kindergarten children, by the end of the school year, are expected to understand that subtraction is a takeaway action. They learn how to make groups of objects from which they take away objects and count how many are left. They also learn to create number sentences such as $10 - 2 = 8$.

You can help your child think about subtraction at an early age by doing things such as holding up two cookies and asking, "If you eat one, how many will be left for me?" Toddlers, preschoolers, and kindergartners enjoy the pictures and rhymes in this book. Play similar subtraction games with your own objects, adapting my rhymes to your setups.

If, when you read the book, you pause at the end of each verse, your child may finish it for you. The rhyme is a clue to the answer. Some children may memorize the rhymes and like to read (or pretend to read) them to you.

As you playfully subtract familiar objects, feel proud that you are starting your child down the path to subtraction!

Happy subtracting,
Jean Marzollo